The Sensible Wedding Planner

*How to Plan
an Unforgettable Celebration
that Is Uniquely Yours*

by
Sarah Brookhaven

Copyright © 2013 Sarah Brookhaven

All rights reserved.

ISBN-13: 978-1483901091
ISBN-10: 1483901092

Acknowledgements

Very special thanks to Danielle Weil and Pegi Dahl for their expertise and help with this book. You ladies are such a joy to work with! Thanks also to John Hope of JohnHopePhotography.com for making the amazing cover photo available on flickr.com (as johnhope14).

Table of Contents

Acknowledgements i

Table of Contents ii

Chapter 1
Redefining the Wedding Fantasy 1

Chapter 2
First Things First – Dream Big 5

    QUIZ: *What Kind of Bride Are You?* 8

    QUIZ RESULTS 10

Chapter 3
Choosing Your Priorities...12

Chapter 4
Consider the Costs
(Or: *HOW* Many Zeros is That?) 16

Chapter 5
Setting Your Budget
(Or: Planning Your Wedding Without Robbing
a Bank) 21

Chapter 6
Getting Organized 26

Chapter 7
In the Planning Trenches
(With Creative Ways to Save) 31

Chapter 8
Bargaining, Bartering, and More 37

Chapter 9
DIY and Other Ways to Save
(Or: Watch Out for that Hot Glue Gun!) 41

Chapter 10
Contingency Planning 49

Chapter 11
Letting off Steam 53

Chapter 12
Coping with Conflicts 59

Chapter 13
Surviving (and Enjoying!) the Big Day 65

Epilogue – You Can Do This! 68

About the Author 69

Chapter 1
Redefining the Wedding Fantasy

What did you want to be when you "grew up?" An Olympic athlete? A doctor? Personally, I wanted to be an astronaut. Or a veterinarian. Or maybe a schoolteacher. It was a tossup, and it changed every day.

The fun part about all your childhood dreams is that, despite how outlandish they may sound, they reveal small pieces of your character – that precious, unique blend of strengths and delights that makes you who you are. So what if you never became that Olympic athlete? I bet you still love sports. Maybe you gave up on the doctor idea in order to become a dentist instead. I'd bet that if you look back at your childhood fantasies, you will find a piece of yourself in every single one.

What about your wedding dreams? Did you ever have any special childhood fantasies about your dream wedding? Who doesn't, right? After all, it's the ultimate romantic dream come true, when you are the belle of the ball, princess for the day, and your Prince Charming is at your side. Think about those childhood dreams for a moment. Were they anything like this?

Two little girls are playing with their dolls. Anna says to Megan, "When I get married, I want a big white dress like this one" (she holds up her Bridal Barbie in her gown). "*I want a big pink vanilla cake covered in roses, and I want to get married in a castle. What do you want at your wedding, Megan?*"

Megan thinks for a minute, twirling a lock of the Barbie's hair. "I want my whole family to be there and everything to be pretty."

Little girls start dreaming about their wedding from a very young age. A quick search at the toy store will show you the "Barbie Every Girl's Dream Wedding" play set, the "Bride and Groom Lego," "Bride and Groom Magnetic Dress-Up" – not to mention all the Disney Princess toys.

When we're little, all these toys, books, and movies plant in our minds the idea of a fantasy "dream wedding" that, if we're lucky enough, we'll get to have when we grow up. The dress, the tiara, and the cake are all part of the package. It's a lovely fantasy that we often forget about as we get older... until it's time to plan our own weddings.

Then, suddenly, we find ourselves engaged, and there are countless decisions to be made: where, when, and *how much to spend*? If you're like Anna, your mind flashes back to everything you dreamed about as a little girl. You sigh over flower arrangements, drool over elaborate 5-tier cakes, and twirl like a princess as you try on dresses, in hopes of finding "the" dress that will transform you into the paragon of dazzling beauty that you dream of being on this special day. And, of course, you go in search of the rustic-yet-elegant castle to hold the ceremony. If only money were no object, you would know exactly what to do.

Or maybe you're more like Megan. She doesn't get bogged down by specifics. She knows she wants to have her family there and for things to be "pretty." I'm sure many of you can relate – you know you want your wedding to be special, but you're not sure of the details.

I assume that if you're reading this, you are engaged. Congratulations! Maybe you're still in the blissful stage of excitement with a goofy – I mean, glowing – grin on your face. Or maybe you've moved on to, "Okay, now *how the heck am I going to plan this wedding?!?!*" Maybe you've even bought a magazine or two. And if you've done that, then you're probably reliving all of your childhood "dream wedding" fantasies... and maybe feeling a bit overwhelmed. Believe me, I've been there. And I learned a lot along the way (sometimes the hard way). That's why I'm writing this book: so that you can learn from my experience and avoid the pitfalls and traps that come with planning a modern wedding.

Whether you're a Megan or an Anna, or anywhere in between, this book is for you. It's here to help you plan your own dream wedding, without breaking the bank or losing your sanity along the way. Your wedding dreams reveal a piece of yourself – your delights, your character – just the way your other childhood fantasies did, and I want to help you discover what will make your wedding truly meaningful and uniquely yours.

The "princess" industry – that, later on, becomes the "wedding industry," – sells us the idea that, in order to feel special, you must feel like a princess, and to feel like a princess, you must have the right dress, venue, cake, flowers, favors, etc. The bridal magazines swarm with gorgeous floral ideas and dreamy pictures of couture wedding dresses, recommending everything from save-the-date cards to adorable wedding favors. Typical wedding planning books and websites bombard you with endless to-do lists, stressing that each step must be handled "just so," because etiquette and tradition say so. It's enough to make your head spin.

So, first things first – *breathe*. Planning a wedding is not nearly as hard as it seems, especially if you are able to "think outside the box" and stay focused on what's really important.

This book is ultimately about discovering that kernel of "you" inside your wedding dreams, so that you can focus on planning the wedding that you really, REALLY want (as opposed to what the princess and wedding industries have told you). Another way to say this – and this may sound sad, but stick with me – is that it's about letting go of the "fantasy" (because, let's face it, most of us can't really afford it) and trading it in for something **even better.** You won't remember many of the details of that day – what it looked like, who was there, what was on the menu – but you will **always** remember what you felt like. More than the dress, the cake, the champagne, or the flowers, the most important thing about your wedding is the person standing right next to you: the person who's about to become your partner for life.

Now, I'm sure you already know that. But, like Anna, it's easy to get bogged down by the details of everything that the wedding industry says you "need" in order to have the perfect wedding. The goal of this book is to keep you focused on the true purpose of your wedding: creating a new family with your groom, while at the same time planning a beautiful celebration that reflects who you are as a couple. And all of that while keeping your sanity, your soul, and your savings intact.

Are you excited? Good! Turn the page, and let's dive in...

Chapter 2
First Things First – Dream Big

Getting married is a Big Deal. Whether you've been together for years and are just now "taking the plunge," whether it's your second wedding, or whether you've only known each other for a short time, your wedding deserves to be a joyous, special, beautiful event. But here's the caveat: I wouldn't call it the "biggest day of your life" as the wedding magazines tend to. A special day? Yes. A memorable one? Of course. But thinking of your wedding as the biggest, most important day of your life sets you up for disappointment. I know this may sound a little harsh, and quite different from what you're used to hearing about weddings, so please let me explain.

Think about it this way: your wedding day is just the *first* day of your marriage. If your wedding is the biggest, most perfect day of your life... well, then what's left for the day after?

Weddings, no matter how big or small, simple or lavish, rarely go as planned. It's a lot easier to go with the flow if you're not so busy making sure everything is perfect. And yet it's also really hard to actually *ruin* a wedding. This should be a comforting thought; no matter what happens, your wedding will not be "ruined." Yes, little things can (and probably will) go wrong, but you can choose not to let it matter. In the end, what truly matters is that you are marrying the person you love. The wedding is just the party that kicks off the adventure that is the rest of your lives together. I don't think weddings should be "perfect." And if you can let go of perfection as well, you will enjoy the planning process, and the wedding itself, a whole lot more.

With that said, it's still important to dream big:

"Always aim for the moon. Even if you miss, you'll land among the stars."
– W. Clement Stone

I think this quotation pretty much sums it up. Now is the time for you to let your imagination run wild. Forget about costs and logistics for a minute and ask yourself: if you could have any kind of wedding, what would it be? Let your heart guide you in the right direction. Now, what makes you smile about these crazy dreams? In other words, what does the experience *feel* like? What do you want to experience on your wedding day? What do you want your guests to feel and experience?

Now is a good point to involve your fiancé in your brainstorming. After all, the wedding isn't a surprise party for the groom. It's something you should be planning together. Even if he's less interested in the minute details, he probably has some ideas about what *he* wants to feel and experience on this important day. So while you're dreaming big, make sure that you're on the same page when it comes to your ultimate vision.

In fact, coming up with this shared vision is a great exercise in compromise – which you'll be doing plenty of during your marriage. You can each take a piece of paper and write down your idea of your dream wedding. They may have some elements in common – and they may be completely different. But if you look for the common themes, and think outside the box, you'll be able to agree on a wedding that fits both of you (more on this in the next chapter).

For now, just focus on the experience, not the details. There will be plenty of time to decide on the details later. Once you have the essence of what you want your wedding experience to be, you can start looking for different (sometimes creative and unconventional) ways to fulfill that vision.

The short, fun quiz on the next page will help you get an idea of what kind of bride you are.

QUIZ: *What Kind of Bride Are You?*

1) *How long have you been planning your wedding?*
   a) Since I was five (remember Anna?). *(1 pt.)*
   b) Since my best friend got married 2 years ago. *(2 pts.)*
   c) Since we got engaged (about 2 weeks). *(3 pts.)*
   d) Haven't really thought about it yet. *(4 pts.)*

2) *How many bridal magazines do you own right now?*
   a) 0 *(4 pts.)*
   b) 1-3 *(3 pts.)*
   c) 4-9 *(2 pts.)*
   d) 10 or more *(1 pt.)*

3) *How do you plan to organize your wedding planning?*
   a) Excel spreadsheet on my smartphone. *(2 pts.)*
   b) Old-fashioned binder with pictures. *(1 pt.)*
   c) A short to-do list in my Gmail. *(3 pts.)*
   d) I need an organizational system? *(4 pts.)*

4) *What did you do the day after getting engaged?*
   a) Went about my day as usual (albeit with a smile on my face the whole time). *(3 pts.)*
   b) Tried on wedding dresses. *(1 pt.)*
   c) Stopped answering my phone because I was so overwhelmed. *(4 pts.)*
   d) Started looking at wedding planning sites. *(2 pts.)*

5) *Who's going dress shopping with you?*
   a) My wedding planner. *(1 pt.)*
   b) My mother. *(2 pts.)*
   c) My fiancé. *(3 pts.)*
   d) I'd rather go by myself. *(4 pts.)*

6) What does your bridal shower look like?
   a) Which one? The lingerie shower, the kitchen shower, or the couples shower? *(1 pt.)*
   b) I'm not having one. *(4 pts.)*
   c) My friends are planning something nice. *(2 pts.)*
   d) An afternoon at the spa with a few close girlfriends. *(3 pts.)*

7) What dishes do you have on your registry?
   a) We didn't put dishes on the registry – we already have them. *(3 pts.)*
   b) A simple pattern that I just fell in love with. *(2 pts.)*
   c) 3 sets: everyday, fancy china, and accent plates. *(1 pt.)*
   d) A registry? I'd rather my guests donate to Greenpeace. *(4 pts.)*

8) What does your dream wedding cake look like?
   a) 3 tiers, coordinated to match the color scheme. *(1 pt.)*
   b) White, simple and delicious. *(2 pts.)*
   c) I'd rather have cupcakes. *(4 pts.)*
   d) My friend is making it for us, and it's a surprise. *(3 pts.)*

9) Who will your bridesmaids be?
   a) Just one: my sister. *(2 pts.)*
   b) All my close friends from high school and college. *(1 pt.)*
   c) I haven't decided yet. *(3 pts.)*
   d) I don't think I need bridesmaids. *(4 pts.)*

Scoring: Add up all the points for your answers.

QUIZ RESULTS

9-13 points: *You're a Perfectionist.*

Like Anna, you've had your wedding planned since you were very young. You have specific ideas about what you want things to look like, so you may need to be careful about getting too attached to any one part of your vision. You may have to fight a tendency to get hung up on the details, so please remember the big picture: what matters is that you get married!

14-22 points: *You're a Traditionalist.*

You probably have an idea of the "traditional" wedding in your head, and you're going to do your best to go along with that. You can (for the most part) keep things in proportion.

23-31 points: *You're a Realist.*

You're a practical thinker who is prepared to compromise easily when it comes to wedding planning. You have a tendency to "go with the flow" and take the path of least resistance – but be careful. You will have to make some decisions when it comes to wedding planning. Don't be afraid to be decisive when it comes to something you really want!

32-36 points: *You're a Non-Conformist.*

Forget about tradition – you're going to do things your way! And that includes tossing out wedding "traditions" like a registry, shower, and cake. If that's what makes you happy, great! The important thing is that you have a wedding that you and your guests enjoy.

You can find more quizzes like this at WeddingBrook.com, where new quizzes are added all the time.

This quiz, while it may seem silly, should give you a good idea of your approach to wedding planning. If you're a non-conformist, it will be easiest for you to be flexible when it comes to your planning decisions. If you scored closer to the perfectionist end of the scale, you may need some time to get used to a different way of thinking. It's important to know yourself and what your expectations are *before* you get started with the planning process. Now it's time to make the transition from big dreams to a more realistic plan.

Chapter 3
Choosing Your Priorities

Now that you've written down your big dreams for your wedding, it's time to decide which of these dreams are *most* important to you – and how you can make them come true. The results of this process will hopefully give your wedding a scale that's grounded in reality and a vibe and feel that remain true to your ultimate vision.

Part of the planning process is realizing that, unfortunately, you just can't have it all. This might be difficult to accept for some brides who have very specific ideas about what they want. On the other hand, it can be incredibly liberating! Instead of feeling like you need to check off every item on those bridal magazine to-do lists, you give yourself permission to worry about only the details that *really matter to you*. This makes for a much more budget-friendly, easier-to-plan wedding – and that means a bride who's less stressed! That's why having a list of your top priorities is so important: so that you know what's non-negotiable and what you're willing to compromise on.

Here's how I recommend you go about this: sit down with your fiancé and your "dream" lists that you made in the previous chapter. You should each go through your own lists and explain what's on your list and why. Circle the things that seem like they could be feasible, or that could work if you changed them a bit.

Then discuss what size you imagine your wedding to be: a large ceremony and reception with all your family and friends? A small courthouse or beach wedding with just family? Or something in between? (It's totally fine if you don't agree at this point: the important thing is to put everything out there.) Now ask yourself why these things will make your wedding special. What is it about that beach wedding that attracts you? Is it the sound of the waves, the open air, the relaxed setting? Or all three? This is the *essence* of the wedding that you're looking to capture. If you can get down to this essence of what you each think your wedding should be , you can build from there, and in the end you will have a wedding that *feels* right for both of you.

Next, choose the vibe you want your wedding to have. The vibe is connected to the *feeling* of the wedding that you're trying to capture. Once you have this down, you can plan the details around it. If you're coming up empty, or have no idea what I'm talking about, here are some words and ideas that may spark your imagination:

Adventurous, elegant, family-oriented, informal, intimate, laid-back, lavish, meaningful, religious, rustic, simple, sophisticated, non-traditional, glamorous, crazy dance party, etc.

Do you get the idea? Don't worry if your "vibes" seem to conflict on the surface. I guarantee you that it's possible to have a simple, sophisticated, rustic, crazy dance party – it will just require some out-of-the-box creative thinking.

Once you've figured out the vibe you want, and the things that are non-negotiable, make achieving that vibe your priority. Write it in big letters and stick it up where you will see it, to remind you of your vision. As you plan, you'll be choosing the details that will help you fulfill that vision – and leaving out the ones that just clutter it all up. If you own a bridal magazine, find one of those pull-out "to-do" checklists. You know, the ones that start two years before the wedding. They're usually conveniently perforated so that you can keep them handy. Pull it out and circle the things that you actually care about in a colored pen. Not the things that you think you need to worry about, but the things that actually matter to *you*. There may be only one item circled, or you may have several.

Now, take another pen (red, if you can find one) and cross off *everything else on the list*. Not because those things don't matter, but because you have just removed them from your list of priorities. You now have permission *not* to care about these details, and when you make decisions about them, it will be a lot easier to do because, ultimately, you've decided that they don't matter for you.

Remember that your wedding is just a ceremony with a celebration attached. It can take any form you want: a garden party, a large church wedding, or a catered event at a hall. It can be as simple or fancy as you want. You can wear a huge dress with a train or a tailored pantsuit. You can have a tiered cake, cupcakes, or an ice cream sundae bar. No matter what you plan, your guests will have a good time, even if it's not the "traditional" wedding they were expecting.

And what about those mysterious animals called "etiquette" and "tradition"? We're told that there's a certain, proper way of doing things, and heaven help you if you ever dare to ignore even one last detail. But here's a reality check for you: "Etiquette" is just another word for being kind, thoughtful, and considerate. Keep that in mind, and you will totally defuse the minefield of etiquette and its myriad faux pas. And those "traditions"? Most of the things we think of as traditions have nothing to do with the traditional weddings of your grandmother's or great-grandmother's time. The traditions are nice, if they are important to you and they fit your budget and your vision. But if they don't, then let me be blunt: don't worry about them. Just like your red-pen list, you can give yourself permission to let them go.

So once you've allowed yourself to let go of the conventional idea of what a wedding should be, and all the "traditions" that you're supposed to follow, you are free to create something entirely different. This is exciting, because it means that you can focus on what will make your wedding unique and special, without feeling overwhelmed and bogged down by everyone else's ideas and conventions. However, on the other hand, when you don't follow the typical wedding formula that's shown in magazines, you suddenly have MANY more options. This can be intimidating. Don't worry. That's what this book is for: to guide you through it, step-by-step.

So, where do you begin? Once you have your lists – your "dream big" list, your "non-negotiable" list, and your "important things/vibe" list – you're ready to move on to the next step: thinking about how much it's all going to cost. If those words are giving you nightmares, let me assure you right now: it will be okay. Turn the page and find out how.

Chapter 4
Consider the Costs
(Or: *HOW* Many Zeros is That?)

Getting married has never been more expensive. The average cost of a wedding in 2012 was $27,000. If you get married in New York, that number skyrockets to $65,000. And these numbers don't include the cost of the honeymoon! Maybe I'm an overly practical person, but I can't imagine spending that amount of money – that I could use to buy a new house or car – on an event that will be over in one day. And yet that's what the wedding industry tells us we need to spend in order to have the "perfect" wedding. Are you beginning to see a pattern? It's no coincidence that putting the word "wedding" or "bridal" on something ramps up the cost. So if you've got unlimited funds, great! But if you're reading this book, chances are you're working within a budget (most people are!) and looking for ways to minimize costs without sacrificing what you want.

If you look through the average wedding planning book or magazine, you'll see a lot of things you didn't even realize you needed! (Hint: You really don't need most of them.) For example:

- ✓ **Sending out engagement announcements or save-the-date cards**. If you absolutely need "save-the-dates," you can use an online invitation service or printing company and have them done for pennies.

- ✓ **Newspaper announcements**. This is another "tradition" that you don't really need.

- ✓ **Engagement gifts.**

- ✓ **Monogrammed cocktail napkins.**

- ✓ **Wedding favors**. These have become very popular recently, but small favors with your names and wedding date can add up to a big unnecessary cost. If having a wedding keepsake for your guests is important to you, you can consider a DIY project or other creative ideas (more in Chapter 9).

- ✓ **Welcome bags**. If you have the time, money, and energy to invest in these, great! If you don't, your guests will not notice they're missing – I promise.

- ✓ **Extra postage**. Check with the USPS to determine which sizes and shapes of envelopes require extra postage, then choose your wedding invitations and other stationery in sizes that use less postage. For example, square invitations are very popular, but they will cost you extra to mail them.

- ✓ **Wedding Announcements**. These are seldom used today.

- ✓ **Formal reception dinner**. A buffet dinner or even hors d'oeuvres can be just as festive (and filling) with much less expense. You will also save on table numbers, wait staff, and seating charts if you have a less formal reception.

Here's a rule of thumb when it comes to paring down all those "extra" expenses: Ask yourself if *you* will notice or care if it's missing from your wedding. If you crossed it off your list with the red pen, then you already know that the answer is "no." Then, ask yourself if your guests will notice if it's missing. If they'll notice, will they care? If it's something like monogrammed napkins, the answer is probably "no." One thing you can definitely cross off the list!

Getting married in America today may be expensive, but it could always be worse. In China, the groom is expected to buy a house and a car for his bride. And when an apartment in Beijing costs 32 times the annual salary of a middle class employee, it's becoming very difficult for many young couples to meet these expectations. In China, "naked weddings" are becoming very popular. I know what you're thinking: *if that means getting married naked, it's not for me* (although it would save a lot of time on dress shopping!). But "naked" just means getting hitched without the house, car and traditional expensive ceremony that's become expected. As one Chinese bride put it, "Every girl wants a romantic wedding, but happiness is more important than anything else. I just want the two of us to be together."

The idea of the "naked wedding" means accepting that you most likely will not be able to afford everything. But before you get too disappointed, remember that this means you will be able to concentrate your time, energy, and resources on the heart and soul of your wedding instead of drowning in the details. Even more than that, a naked wedding means realizing that weddings *shouldn't have to be so expensive.* It means shifting the focus from the "pomp and circumstance" of the ceremony to what's really important: sharing your happiness with the people you care about, and celebrating the creation of a new family with your partner.

Here's a gentle reality check: it's impossible to get married for free these days. Even the simplest courthouse wedding includes a charge for the marriage license and registration fees. And if you want to have a party or a reception with guests, even a self-catered affair will require buying food. So here are some general guidelines for wedding costs: If you have more guests, your wedding will cost more. If you have more attendants, you're also looking at higher costs. The most expensive part of your wedding is likely to be the reception. These three elements are what contribute most to the expense of the wedding. If you can find ways to scale back a bit when it comes to your guest list, attendants, and reception, you can slash your budget by a significant amount. Of course, if these elements are non-negotiables, there are plenty of other ways to get creative and save on costs (which we'll be talking about in later chapters – stay tuned!)

You can never really have quick, low-budget, and luxury all at once. The most you can aim for is two out of three. For example, if you want to put together a high-end wedding in a short amount of time, it's going to cost more. If you want to do it quickly on a low budget, you may not get your first choices on many things. And if you want a high-end wedding on a low budget, it's going to take time to plan and get all the details in place.

This is where many people will ask: What about Do-It-Yourself? Won't that save us lots of money? The short answer is: yes, it will save you money. But it might not be worth it in the long run. DIY requires a lot more time and know-how, and is a lot more stressful than hiring someone else to do it for you. Some things are great for DIY (like making your own playlist instead of hiring a band). Self-catering the whole reception, on the other hand, is not something to be taken lightly. Before you take on a DIY project, consider ALL the costs in terms of time, stress, supplies, etc. We'll talk a lot more about DIY in a later chapter. For now, if you or someone you know has a special talent and can possibly volunteer their time to DIY, write it down.

Now it's time to go into some practical specifics about setting your budget. I'm about to show you how you can take advantage of *all* your assets (not just the ones in the bank) to maximize your budget and get the ball rolling on your wedding plans.

Chapter 5
Setting Your Budget
(Or: Planning Your Wedding Without Robbing a Bank)

We've already mentioned how much the typical wedding costs. If you don't remember, it was a healthy five figures. Now it's time to talk about how much *your* wedding is going to cost. Because I know how daunting it can be, I've broken down the budgeting process into the following steps:

Step One: *Research*

While researching prices for venues, catering, and everything else can be *very* scary, it's important to know what the average wedding prices are for your area. Call around or Google local venues, caterers, photographers, bakeries, etc. to get a feel for the price ranges. This initial research will give you an indication of where you may have to get creative and make compromises if things are way out of your budget.

Step Two: *Figure Out Who's Paying*

Have your parents already offered to help with the wedding? Do they want to contribute something but don't have the funds? Or are you financing the whole shebang by yourselves? I know it's unpleasant to talk about money, *especially* with your parents and in-laws, but having these conversations now can save you a lot of uncomfortable and awkward situations later on when it comes time to pay the bills.

If your parents offer to help, you should understand that they will probably want some part in the decision making process. They are investing large sums of money into this – it's understandable that they may take an interest in how the money is being spent. On the other hand, it is *your* wedding, not theirs, and you may feel that you and your fiancé should have final veto power.

Talk to them about the elements of the wedding that are important to them. If those elements are on your "non-essential" list, then you can be flexible and include them in the process. If they're "non-negotiables" be up front about this, and calmly explain that A, B, and C are very important to you, and kindly request that the ultimate decisions for these things be left up to you and your fiancé. (For more on negotiating with family, see Chapter 12.)

Step Three: *Figure Out Your Budget*

Taking into account what your parents may be offering and the amount that you can reasonably afford, come up with a final number of how much you can afford to spend. Don't worry if this number is significantly lower than the "average" of $27,000 we talked about. It's possible to plan a beautiful wedding for $10,000, $5,000 or even $1,000 – IF you calculate your assets properly.

Step Four: *Calculate* ALL *Your Assets*

I'm not just talking about money here. Even with a small budget, you have a lot more resources than you think. Consider the following: how much time do you have to plan and invest in preparations? This is an asset. Write it down. How much energy will you have for planning? Energy is also a valuable resource.

Who's going to help you? Friends, family, friends of family, family of friends – you get the picture. Your social connections have their own talents and resources of their own, and most of them want to help. If someone has already volunteered to help with something specific, write it down (for example, your cousin owns a bakery and she wants to make your cake, or your best friend knows a florist who will give you a good discount). This will be helpful later in the planning process. You should likewise make a list of your own special skills and talents, even if these skills have nothing to do with wedding planning. Many vendors may be willing to work on a barter system if you have something valuable to offer, or you may choose to do some things yourself.

This list will help you when it comes to the next step...

Step Five: *Allocate Resources*

It's better to do a few things well than to do a lot of things poorly. You already have your list of the elements of your wedding that are most important to you. These are the elements that should consume a greater portion of your resources (notice how I didn't write "money," because now we know your resources include more than just money!). On the other hand, don't confuse "more expensive" with "better." Just because something costs more doesn't mean it will ultimately be the best choice. For example, your mother's wedding dress, with a few alterations, may be a better fit for you than choosing a new, expensive gown.

You shouldn't feel pressured to spend money if something makes you financially uncomfortable. You don't "have to" spend a certain amount on anything, and you certainly don't have to do anything that doesn't feel right to you. If you're talking about something like chairs, which you probably don't care much about but will most likely need to have, you can either go with the most basic rentals or look for other solutions. Something to remember: *if you can think creatively, there is always another option – and it will most likely save you money.*

Don't let the "etiquette" and "tradition" monsters take over your budget either. Do what's right for you as a couple and free yourself from the bounds of "tradition." If certain traditions work for you and your fiancé, then by all means embrace them!

Step Six: *Get Organized*

We'll be talking a lot more about how to stay organized in a later chapter. For now, you can draw up a rough budget: a list of elements, vendors, etc. in one column, and the cost/how it's being paid for in another. It may be a monetary amount, or it may read: "cake: Anna," "dress: Mom's, alterations $200." Just get as much as you can on paper. This includes the small details that will add up, like postage stamps for invitations, tips for the waiters, etc.

Since most projects do go over budget, give yourself some breathing room. Put an extra 10-15% in the budget as a "just in case" fund. Some experts even suggest as much as 20% for unexpected expenses. For example, if your budget is $15,000 for your entire wedding, set aside as much as $3,000 for those surprise costs. Aim for the lower number – in the example that would be $12,000 – but don't feel bad if you need the extra for last-minute expenses. That's what it's there for! And believe me, you will probably need it.

A final word on budgets: If you spend an amount of money that seems reasonable to you, and your wedding is the beautiful and special experience that you hoped for, you will feel like it was money well spent. If you have "buyer's remorse" after the wedding for the amount that you spent, well, the wedding is over, it was amazing, and you can't un-spend the money now, can you? But you will also never have to spend that money ever again. And you can breathe a huge sigh of relief about that... and enjoy your honeymoon!

For even more suggestions about how to make the most of your wedding budget, be sure to check out all the ideas and tips at WeddingBrook.com.

Now that you've got a budget, it's time to dive in to planning – and that includes looking for ways to "think outside the box" and save money.

Chapter 6
Getting Organized

There's no getting around it: you <u>will</u> need some kind of organizational system. No matter how small your wedding may be – unless you're eloping to the Elvis Chapel in Las Vegas – you will need to do some planning. And things will go a lot more smoothly on the day itself if you have everything organized from the very beginning. So it's time to channel your inner OCD (just a little bit) and find a system that works for you to keep things in order.

What if you're not the organized type? Every bride is different. Every couple is different. Every wedding is different. And there is a plethora of different ways to organize a wedding. Some of the popular options include:

1) Post-its and piles of paper kept in a folder. Some creative minds work best when things appear to be disorganized – but they know exactly where everything is.

2) A binder divided by subject, with lots of room to paste in pictures clipped from magazines for inspiration. If you're the old-school type and have lots of wedding magazines, this system may work best for you. You may want to create separate folders for the ceremony, flowers, music, cakes, venues, caterers, and wedding dresses.

3) Online all-in-one planners that have smartphone apps so that you can keep track of everything from your phone. These apps will keep track of your budget, registry, seating chart, guest list, and more. Other apps can color-coordinate, keep a "flip book" of your wedding dress favorites, and search for honeymoon packages. If you can't live without your smartphone, there's a good chance you'll find some of these apps very useful. But, just like with wedding magazines, don't get so caught up in the details that you lose sight of your ultimate vision.

4) The spreadsheet system. Spreadsheets give you one central place where you can enter and sort information, and share it with whoever needs it. Chances are you will need separate sections, spreadsheets, or folders for different parts of the wedding. Here's how I'd break it down. (Of course, you can do whatever works best for you and your wedding.)

- ✓ **Guest list and RSVP.** (It's helpful to include guest emails and addresses here, too.)

- ✓ **Who's in charge of doing what.** This will help you and your fiancé in the early planning stages, too.

- ✓ **Vendor contacts.** You'll be doing quite a bit of research, and it will be handy to have everyone's contact information in one place.

- ✓ **Wedding Week:** Hotel and flight information for out-of-town guests, etc.

- ✓ **The Weekend Before:** This should list all the events leading up to the wedding, what needs to happen, who's in charge of doing what, etc.

✓ **Wedding Day Spreadsheet:** Every activity that will take place on your wedding day, with a time, location, and a person selected to be in charge (see Chapter 9 for more about choosing that all-important day-of coordinator).

You may find you need all of these lists and more. You may find that some of them are unnecessary. Again, it's all about adapting and finding the tools that work best for you. Be sure to check out WeddingBrook.com for even more information and ideas about organizational systems and which ones work best for you.

And that brings us to another big decision: should you hire a wedding planner?

Do you need a wedding planner? It depends. Some couples will do just fine planning the wedding on their own. Others may find it money well spent to hire a wedding planner who will keep them organized, calm, and on track. A good wedding planner wears many hats: diplomat, psychologist, gal-pal, style consultant, and, most of all, organizer.

Although a wedding planner is a significant expense, you may get some return on your investment, as they can sometimes use their connections to find you better deals than you could find on your own. A wedding planner will also help you understand what's realistic for your budget, and help you stick to your budget. If you know that you tend to overspend, you may appreciate having a professional to keep you on track. If you go with a full-service wedding planner, they will be handling all the details from the planning stages to the big day. Alternately, you can hire a partial event planner to give you advice and vendor recommendations on an hourly basis. A day-of coordinator may be another alternative, if you prefer to do the planning yourself but need someone to keep the big day running smoothly.

You should consider hiring a wedding planner if:

- ✓ You are having a **large wedding** (over 200 guests).

- ✓ You have **difficult family dynamics** that will make planning by yourself difficult.

- ✓ Your **work schedule** doesn't leave extra time to devote to planning.

- ✓ You have an **organizational phobia**. I mean serious "I can't even look at this stuff" fear. If the thought of wedding planning terrifies you, then a wedding planner may be worth every penny just for your peace of mind.

If you do choose to hire a wedding planner, make sure all the terms in the contract are clear, and that you know exactly what you are getting for the fee. Be sure to ask what is and isn't included in the fee. And before you hire someone, check their references and get recommendations from friends. Another important factor in choosing a wedding planner is if this person is on board with your ultimate wedding vision. Are they likely to make you more or less stressed when it comes to making decisions and thinking outside the box? Are they likely to have you do things "their way," or can they be flexible with some of the arrangements? You shouldn't underestimate the power of a personal connection and a good relationship. If you don't have good chemistry with your wedding planner, the next few months are likely to be miserable – so choose wisely.

The biggest benefit of a wedding planner is that you can delegate most, if not all, of the organization. Your wedding planner will be the one with the binder and files, and all you have to do is make the decisions. It can be quite a relief for a stressed-out bride to have someone to entrust with the planning process. Of course, it's up to you to choose how much you want to delegate.

There are certain circumstances where the benefits of having a wedding planner justify the cost. But does that mean that you **need** a wedding planner? No, not really. As long as you have some kind of organizational system that works for you, you **can** plan this wedding yourself. Once you've gotten organized, it's time to enter the planning trenches and start filling up those binders, folders, and spreadsheets with your wedding details!

Chapter 7
In the Planning Trenches
(With Creative Ways to Save)

It's planning time! Are you excited? This is when your vision and your budget start to take the shape of something resembling a wedding. You'll be deciding the What, When, Where, Who, and How of your wedding – and I'll be helping you with creative ways to save money and maximize your assets along the way. Plus, don't forget to check out WeddingBrook.com for even more money-saving suggestions.

When it comes to modern wedding planning, it can seem like your options are endless – and that can make decisions difficult. With so many options, even the smallest details can seem important. That's why we've prepared our lists and (hopefully) gotten the message that *nothing about wedding planning is a life-or-death decision.* Each decision you make brings you one step closer to being married. And if these decisions are on your red-pen list, then they don't really matter. Just choose something. And then cross it off your list. It feels good, and it frees you up to spend more time making the decisions that *do* matter to you.

Remember when we said your wedding day *isn't* the biggest day of your life? Well, here's a friendly reminder. And that means that when you're making decisions, "good" is usually good enough. If you wait and wait to make a decision because you're still weighing your options, you may miss out on a good choice, or the prices may go up while you deliberate. So no, you won't be making perfect choices all the time. But if they feel right and they make you happy, they will be good enough. And that's what really matters. Some decisions are pretty important, however, and we're going to cover those right now.

Decision #1: *Picking a Date*

There are many factors that go into choosing a wedding date. Venue availability and family and personal schedules may limit you a bit. But here are some other things to consider when choosing a date:

- ✓ **Avoid dates within 2 weeks of a holiday if at all possible**. Logistically, it makes things more complicated for your guests in terms of travel and hotel stays.

- ✓ **Consider the season**. June and July are the busiest wedding months – and the most expensive. Getting married "off-season" can save you a bundle of money on the venue – and everything else. When you choose your month, take into account the weather of the region you live in. A winter wedding if you live in a snowy climate will have its own challenges. Spring or fall may be better options, but depending where you live the weather may be unpredictable.

- ✓ **Weekday weddings are always less expensive**. They're also more difficult for your guests to attend, so keep in mind that if you do choose to get married on a weekday, your wedding may be smaller. If you're aiming for a small wedding, choosing a weekday could work to your advantage.

- ✓ **Time of day**: evening weddings that include a sit-down dinner are the most expensive. Moving the ceremony to late morning or afternoon is cheaper, and it gives you more options in terms of the food that you can serve (think brunch, desserts, potluck, and more).

Decision #2: *Choosing the Venue*

This decision should really be made together with choosing a date. If you want to book a specific venue, that may limit your date options, and vice versa. But you can also think outside the box and choose an "unconventional" venue. Just a few ideas to consider: a national park, a church or community social hall, your own home, or a friend's house or garden. I've even heard of one couple who saw a scenic meadow with a gorgeous view while out taking a drive. They stopped to ask the owners of the farm if they could use the meadow for their wedding, and they discovered that they could "rent" the meadow (including accommodations for parking) for much less than a typical venue in the area. Another couple had their hearts set on a beautiful beach wedding with a specific lighthouse in the background, but the cost of rental for the beach and grounds around the lighthouse was prohibitive. They discovered a public park on the opposite side of the lighthouse (but still on the beach) with an extraordinarily cheap rental cost. The beloved lighthouse was still the beautiful backdrop for their wedding, but without the exorbitant cost of renting the lighthouse grounds specifically. Your venue will really set the tone of your wedding, so it should be somewhere that you feel comfortable. On the other hand, don't feel that you should overlook some of the so-called "budget" options. I've seen so many amazingly beautiful, creative and unique weddings that were held in someone's backyard garden or a church social hall.

Decision #3: *The Guest List*

How big or small is your wedding going to be? Maybe you're sure you want an intimate ceremony with just close friends and family. Maybe you'd like to invite everyone you know. Your actual guest list will probably fall somewhere in between. You and your fiancé should sit down and list everyone you'd like to invite. You can also have your parents make a list of people who absolutely must receive an invitation.

To break down the guest list, I recommend making a few separate lists: (1) close family and friends, (2) family and friends, and (3) acquaintances who should probably get an invite. If you end up with a total number you can manage given your budget, great! If not, you will have to cut some people. You might feel that someone "should" get an invitation for tradition's sake or some other reason – these are the people that will probably not make the cut.

Decision #4: *What's for Dinner?*

Food is a central component of a wedding reception. But that doesn't mean you need the "traditional" three-course sit-down dinner to please your guests. And at the rates most caterers charge, food is by far one of the most expensive aspects of a wedding. That means you will save your biggest chunk of money by choosing not to have a sit-down catered dinner. Here are some other options:

- ✓ **You can arrange for the food and beverages yourself, and hire a staff of local students to serve**. Posting on Craigslist can get you a wide range of responses, but there are also companies that will connect you with students looking for gigs.

- ✓ **Buffet-Style**: If you choose to have a buffet, you won't need nearly as many waiters, and guests will be able to choose what and how much they want to eat. One bride I know actually served a pizza buffet at her wedding, and in a very pretty way.

- ✓ **Hors d'oeuvres/Dessert reception**: This is a great option if you're having a wedding earlier in the day and don't want to serve a full meal. Dessert is the best part of the meal anyway, right? You can also go to Costco or Sam's Club and stock up on hors d'oeuvres, or serve a light brunch instead of a large meal.

- ✓ **Potluck**: This is another creative option. Instead of asking your guests to bring a gift, have them bring a dish, instead. This option works best if you're having a small wedding.

- ✓ **Self-catering**: Yes, you *can* cater your wedding yourself. That doesn't mean slaving over the hot stove all by yourself. You can recruit friends and relatives to contribute dishes, or you can choose to cater only part of the meal. If you feel confident enough, you can choose to go "all the way."

Once these decisions have been made, you will start to feel that your wedding is emerging from the world of dreams and lists into reality. Now you know when and where you're getting married! Take a moment to be excited about that, because it means a big part of the hard decision-making is behind you.

Remember, as you're doing your research for venues and catering, don't be afraid to consider "outside the box" options, and don't be afraid to negotiate or ask for discounts. As my mother always says, "You don't ask, you don't get!" If the thought of driving a hard bargain makes you mildly nauseous, here are some tips: Keep in mind that vendors are *expecting* you to negotiate. They have likely built this into their quote already, which means that they've already planned to give you some kind of discount – all you have to do is ask! Also, flattery works wonders. Practice saying: "We really love this, but we are on a tight budget. Maybe we can customize this package so that it works for both of us?" And don't forget to ask if the vendor would be willing to barter for a service you can provide. The bottom line is that it never hurts to ask. And the more you practice the art of negotiation, the easier it will become. By the time you're done planning your wedding, you will be an expert in negotiating and getting bargains.

So after you've chosen your date and venue, finalized the guest list and decided what food will be served, it's time to move to the next stage of planning – and to get your friends and family involved!

Chapter 8
Bargaining, Bartering, and More

In this chapter, we'll cover different ways of getting what you want for your wedding without spending a fortune. These include asking for discounts, barter opportunities, and recruiting family and friends to help. It's all about "maximizing your assets" and learning to take advantage of the resources that you already have available: your own skills and talents, and those of your friends and family. Remember that your wedding budget isn't only the amount of money you have in the bank. You have lots of resources that you can draw from, if you know how to make the most of them.

We talked about negotiating for discounts in the previous chapter. Again, don't be afraid to speak up. What's the worst that could happen? Someone will say "no"? It's much more likely that they'll say yes, especially if you are working with a smaller vendor or your wedding is planned for one of the "off-season" times we discussed (weekdays, mornings, or winter). The word "negotiation" often conjures up images of sleazy car salesmen and Hollywood-style money deals. But if you approach it in a friendly way, successful negotiation doesn't have to be sleazy or awkward. Here are some tips that may help you as you negotiate:

✓ **Remember to keep your head high and smile.** Be friendly, confident, and positive.

- ✓ **Compliment the vendor's work.** For example, if you're negotiating for a cake, tell them that you love a specific technique that they've used.

- ✓ **Be sure to use the person's name – it helps.** Just don't overdo it.

- ✓ **Ask open-ended questions.** Instead of saying, "Do you offer a discount on this package?" try: "What is your discount for this package?"

- ✓ **Don't talk too much.** Ask for what you want and then give them a chance to think about it and respond.

- ✓ **Just go for it!** Remember my mother's motto: "You don't ask, you don't get!"

If you can't negotiate a discount – or if the discount isn't enough and you really have your heart set on a specific cake, dress or centerpiece – consider offering something to barter. If you're saying to yourself, "I don't have anything to barter," then think again. What are you good at? What is your partner good at? If you have trouble thinking of anything, ask your friends and family what they think. They may have some creative ideas about skills you can barter, or they may offer some of their own special talents for you to barter (more about recruiting friends and family later).

If you own your own business, or if you have a special talent, then you have a built-in bartering tool. Therapists, accountants, lawyers, shop owners, photographers, teachers, graphic designers – just about any specialized profession or business will have something to offer. Do you play an instrument or speak another language? You can offer lessons to the vendor or their family in exchange. Is your partner a wiz at building websites? Offer to build a customized new site for their business. The options are endless, if you can think creatively and value **all** your skills and talents.

Keep in mind that, when you barter, you may need to compromise and negotiate a deal that's beneficial for both parties. You'll also need lots of patience, as it may take you time to find a vendor that's willing to barter. Be sure to check each vendor's references, and expect that they will check yours as well. After all, you want to know something about whom you're trading with!

One more important thing: get **everything** in writing. While it may seem more casual than money trading hands – and while it may feel awkward to ask – bartering is a transaction, just like paying cash or writing a check. It's important to have a signed contract and receipts so that everyone is clear about who's providing what.

There are several websites devoted to helping people barter wedding items. You sign up and post what you have to offer, and search for what you need. These websites put you in direct contact with people who are already looking to barter, so you don't have to convince anyone. You will also reach more people than if you approach individual vendors by yourself. Another option is to go through a commercial barter service. The advantage to these is that you can barter with any member of the exchange and earn credits for the things you need, as opposed to negotiating one-on-one deals by yourself. If you choose to use a website, please be careful and take precautions. It's a sad fact that not everyone on the internet can be trusted. For more information about bartering services and websites, check out WeddingBrook.com.

If you're trying to plan your wedding without breaking the bank, it's a good idea to take all the help that's offered from friends and family. You may feel like it's "your" wedding, and that by accepting help you will somehow lose control or it will become less "yours." It's understandable to feel that way, but it's also important to remember that your wedding isn't just about you and your partner tying the knot. It's about sharing this special event with the people who love and care about you, who may feel like they want to help and contribute to your wedding. They're excited for your wedding and if they know you're on a budget, they're probably looking to help you out in any way they can. By allowing them to help, you are allowing them to love you and share in a part of your wedding magic. If you keep that in mind, then it will be easier for you to accept their offers graciously, without feeling guilty. They say it takes a village to raise a child, and while it may not take a whole village to plan a wedding, by accepting favors from family and friends you allow them to contribute their own personal touch and give special meaning to your wedding day.

Chapter 9
DIY and Other Ways to Save
(Or: Watch Out for that Hot Glue Gun!)

For many people, the term "do-it-yourself" (also known as DIY) brings to mind a whole host of artsy, craftsy, get-your-hands-dirty types of projects. And yes, there is definitely a side of DIY that includes those fun activities. But DIY doesn't have to mean getting messy with the glue gun – you'd be surprised at all the aspects of the wedding that you can DIY without one!

If you are looking for ways to save money on your wedding (and who isn't?), then DIY is an option you should definitely explore. There are plenty of DIY ideas at WeddingBrook.com. Plus, by handling some details of the wedding yourself (or better yet, by doing it together with your fiancé or your friends), you can add a very personal touch to the wedding and create some precious memories in the process. You don't even need to be creative, handy, or artsy to save some money with DIY. The trick is to choose the details that you and your loved ones can handle with grace, ease, and – above all else – fun.

However, before you take on **any** DIY projects, make sure that you don't overextend yourself or your loved ones. DIYing a bunch of projects for your wedding can become a big burden very quickly, and may pile too many demands on an already stressful event. The key here is **moderation.** By choosing specific, meaningful elements, DIY can be incredibly rewarding. This chapter will show you how to DIY in a sensible, realistic, and cost-effective way, without making yourself – or your loved ones – crazy.

At first glance, DIY sounds like a great way to save money on your wedding. The reality? Not always. If you're attempting a complicated project that you don't have experience with, you may end up spending more money on supplies than you would have spent just hiring someone to do it for you – not to mention wasting your valuable time. So before you start **any** DIY project, ask yourself the following: Is this a non-negotiable must-have for our wedding? Can we afford to hire someone to do it? If not, is it something that we can realistically do ourselves and still stay on budget? If DIY is not the cheaper option, then you should have no qualms about hiring someone to do it – unless it's a specific project that's very important to you.

The obvious reason to DIY is to save money, and in many cases it does significantly cut costs. But the *best* reason to DIY? Because you enjoy it. Don't DIY because you think it will make your wedding somehow better to have handcrafted centerpieces and favors, or because you think you need to jump on the DIY bandwagon. Here's the bottom line: DIY isn't always better. But it is **always** more time consuming. Every project you choose to DIY will take time, and part of choosing your DIY projects wisely is thinking about your time as a valuable resource and asset. With that in mind, don't take on more than you can handle in the time you have. Most DIY projects usually take 50-100% longer than you think they will, so take this into account when you plan your time. Don't forget to order extra materials to allow for mistakes – ordering an extra 10% is usually enough without ending up with way too much left over.

I've found that the best way to DIY is not to do it yourself, but to do it **together.** You should consider asking and allowing your loved ones to help you. If you make your DIY activities a fun experience – for example, having a party with your bridesmaids to make wedding favors – you will have those memories of a fun experience to savor, in addition to the favors themselves.

Here are some ideas to help you (and your family and friends) DIY in a practical and fun way:

1) **Invitations.** Invitations are one of those things that can easily save you a few hundred dollars if you DIY. You have a few options to DIY invitations:

- ✓ **Have an artistic friend design your invitation**, whether it's hand-crafted or a graphic design on the computer. Then you can either print them yourself or use an inexpensive online printing service.

- ✓ **Get a group of friends together** to make scrapbook-style invitations. Each one will be unique, and you'll have lots of fun making them!

- ✓ The **free option:** One idea that is gaining popularity is to ditch the formal paper invitations altogether and use social media and email to get the word out about your wedding. There are plenty of free websites that will let you design your own invitations and keep track of RSVPs entirely online. Almost everyone has email these days, and it's environmentally friendly to save on paper, too! For Great-Grandma and those holdouts that don't have email, you can have a few invitations printed up and sent via snail mail.

2) **Music.** Who says you need a 5-piece wedding band? You may not even need a DJ. In the age of digital music

and the iPod, you can easily create your own customized playlist of wedding music. To successfully DJ your own wedding, you'll need two things: the right amplification system and a friend to help. Look into renting an affordable professional amplification system that you can run with a computer – people need loud music to keep up the energy of a fun dance party. You'll also want to appoint a "playlist bouncer" who is in charge of the computer – keeping the music going, dealing with any technical issues, and switching songs if they see that nobody's dancing.

Be sure to fill your playlist with songs that people know and like. You can mix in the songs that are important to you and your partner, but music that your guests love will keep them on the dance floor and having fun. Mix up genres and generations, so that there's a little something for everyone to enjoy. Don't forget to cross-fade your playlist so that one song flows into another and there's no pause in between. Once you've picked the songs, think about the flow of the party when you put your playlist in order. Follow a few fast songs with a slow song, and save the nostalgic party favorites for the end when everyone's really into it. Oh, and don't forget to pick a great song for your first dance as a married couple!

3) Photography. With today's technology, it seems like everyone has a nice professional camera. This means that you can actually turn your wedding guests into your photographers. If you choose to go this route, you can either choose a smaller package from a professional wedding photographer, or go without one entirely. Just make sure that you ask your friends-with-cameras in advance if they'd be willing to help. It's best to find a core group of guests who are excited to take pictures and create a plan so that different people are responsible for different parts of the wedding day. Dividing up the responsibilities means that the important parts will be photographed, and your guests can still relax and enjoy most of the party. Another good tip is to write out a shot list. You'd be awfully disappointed if you realized after the fact that no one captured a picture of you smashing cake in your husband's face. So make a list of the moments that you want to capture, and if you want formal family pictures as well, list all the people and combinations that you'd like. This way you'll be sure not to miss anything.

4) Flowers. Unlike music and photography, flowers require a bit more skill and planning to DIY. If you're not the Martha Stewart type you may just want to stick with bouquets. Bouquets are fairly simple and straightforward, and you can find lots of tutorials and videos online showing you how to make them. If you have some experience and want to go all out and DIY all the flowers, you'll need to put some more time and energy into planning and logistics. If you decide to use real flowers, keep in mind that you'll have to do everything the day or two before the wedding, when things are very hectic. Be sure to use gloves – roses and other flowers with thorns can nick your hands and ruin your manicure. If you have a friend or family member that's good with flowers, don't hesitate to ask them for help. Remember the motto: Do it together.

5) Dress. If you think that all there is to dress shopping is walking into a bridal store, trying on a few, and picking one, think again! Sure, that's an option, but you have many other choices when it comes to your gown, including DIY. And before you hyperventilate just thinking about making a wedding gown, let me tell you that there are lots of ways to DIY without ever touching a needle or thread. You can recycle a dress that was your mother's, grandmother's, or a friend's. You can buy a white bridesmaid's dress or a prom dress and save money that way. You can buy a used dress on ebay or Craigslist for a fraction of the price. You can also choose the full-on DIY option and make or alter your own dress, if you have the sewing chops and that sounds like a fun project to you. Or, if you're feeling very unconventional, you can choose not to wear a wedding gown and wear something else that makes you feel comfortable, special, and most of all – like YOU.

6) Attendants and their attire. As far as wedding attendants are concerned, the most important factor to consider is what's important to you and your fiancé. Don't let tradition put you in a box. For example, here are some "traditions" that I'd like to debunk right now: First of all, you don't need matching numbers of attendants.   Your attendants do not need matching outfits or expensive gifts. And heck, you don't even need attendants at all! You can choose to have just a maid of honor, or your best guy friend as a "man of honor." You can have 10 color-coordinated bridesmaids if you wish. Or you can choose something in between. But don't feel like you have to commit to the expensive matching bridesmaids' dresses and gifts. One nice way to DIY and save on dresses is to let each bridesmaid wear her favorite "little black dress." Or pick a color and let them find their own dress in that color. If you're concerned that the dresses might not match – not all fuchsias are the same – you can buy half a yard of fabric in the color of your choice, and give each attendant a swatch to use while dress-shopping. As for gifts for your attendants, a heartfelt note and a small present can be much more meaningful than an expensive piece of jewelry. Go with your instincts and do what feels right to you.

7) Catering. Catering is one of those big things that you should only attempt to DIY if you know you can successfully pull it off – and enjoy it. Do you throw dinner parties? Do you know how to cook? Does cooking make you happy? If so, you can think about self-catering. If not, it is just not worth the time, effort, and stress to attempt a DIY on this one. Trust me. While catering is a big expense, there are other ways to save than self-catering: by doing a dessert reception, hors d'oeuvres instead of a big meal, a potluck, etc.

8) Serving Dishes. Before you buy, ask your friends and family members if they'd be willing to loan you extra flatware, platters, bowls, and glasses. Many people have extra sets that they never use that they'd be happy to let you borrow. Just make sure that you don't borrow things that are irreplaceable or valuable – accidents do happen, and you don't want to have to explain to Aunt Millie why she no longer has her favorite serving platter.

9) Decorations. One of the easiest areas to DIY is with decorations. Check Craigslist and Ebay for couples selling their decorations. Thrift stores may also carry décor items that will fit your wedding vibe. This is also an area where your artsy, crafty talents can come into play. Just remember to have fun with it and keep it simple.

No matter how much or little you choose to DIY, the one thing you should NOT try to DIY is the wedding day itself. You don't want to spend your wedding day running around with checklists – you want to enjoy your special day! Even if you don't hire a wedding planner, you might want to consider hiring a professional wedding coordinator for the actual wedding day – someone to make sure all the details are handled so that you and your closest family and friends can relax and enjoy the day. If that's not a possibility, then you will want to choose one or two people you can trust to be your wedding managers. The wedding managers will be very busy and preoccupied all day, so be sure to ask only those people who will not mind missing out on the wedding experience.

If you choose two people, one can coordinate the ceremony and the other can handle the reception. They can also work as a team. Make sure the people you choose know what they're getting into, and that they're the types who thrive on organization, and running the show. They should be people who are up for a challenge, as they will have to take charge of the entire day and deal with any issues that may pop up.

Make time to meet with your managers before the wedding, giving each a copy of the vendor lists and a schedule for the day. Go over the information so that everyone's clear on who should be doing what and when. If you've chosen to DIY any aspect of the food, cake, flowers, or other projects, you will have to plan on how to transport these things to the wedding itself. Be sure to think about the logistics of keeping everything cool and stable during transport. Make a list of everything the managers are responsible for, so that there are no surprises. And once you've done that, **trust them.** You won't be able to enjoy the wedding if you're worried about what's going on behind the scenes.

The most important thing to remember about DIY and weddings is not to overextend yourself or your closest friends and family. Especially on the day of the wedding, you and your friends and family should be free to savor the moment.

Chapter 10
Contingency Planning

When planning any big event, it's important to have backup and contingency plans for when things go wrong. All the more so when it comes to your wedding! Being flexible but realistic can save your wedding and save you stress.

In the commercial aircraft industry, even the safest parts of the plane have double- or even triple-backup systems, just in case the primary system stops working. It's not because the primary system is likely to fail; it's because *if* the primary system ever *does* fail, the consequences would be disastrous. And while I'm not going to compare your wedding to a plane crash – it is next to impossible to actually ruin a wedding, after all – it *is* a special (and expensive) once-in-a-lifetime event. While the big things aren't likely to go wrong, if they did the whole event could become much more stressful. So you'll need to have backup plans in place to cover that "just in case" that you'd rather not think about.

Many couples are choosing to purchase wedding insurance. This can give you peace of mind, knowing that your wedding will go on no matter what, and to protect the financial investment that you're making. There are two main types of insurance: event insurance and liability insurance.

Event insurance means that your investments are protected against extreme situations that might cause postponement (severe weather, accident, sudden illness) and against financial loss if the event goes on but you have a glitch along the way (no-show vendors, lost photographs, damage to the wedding gown, etc.). You should consider getting event insurance if:

- ✓ You're worried about **recovering your deposits** if a vendor goes bankrupt or doesn't deliver as promised.

- ✓ You're concerned that **extreme weather** or an **unexpected illness** or injury could force you to postpone.

- ✓ The bride or groom is **in the military** and approved leave could be cancelled.

Liability insurance protects you if you're held responsible for alcohol-related accidents, property damage, or bodily injury at your wedding or arising from it. This type of insurance is now required by many venues, so be sure to check with your venue to see if it's required. Liability insurance will cover your behind if something should happen to one of your guests, or if damage should occur to the venue as a result of your wedding. But if you've chosen a non-traditional venue, and your wedding budget is small, you may choose not to purchase insurance – and that's fine too. You can find more information about wedding insurance at WeddingBrook.com.

Whether or not you purchase insurance, you will need to have contingency plans for the most important parts of the wedding. What are the "important" parts, you may ask? Ask yourself this question: "How would I feel if the _____ (cake, dress, flowers, photographer, etc.) didn't show up?" If the answer makes you hyperventilate, you should probably have a contingency plan for that part of the wedding:

- ✓ **If your venue is outdoors**, make sure you have an indoor backup in case of inclement weather.

- ✓ **Consider having a list of alternate vendors** that you can call at the last minute if your vendors cancel or disappear. This is a distant possibility, but it's always good to have backup.

- ✓ **If your officiant gets sick or can't make it**, make sure you have someone else you can count on to show up if needed.

- ✓ **Many of the DIY options discussed in Chapter 9 can serve as backup plans as well**. Even if you have a DJ or a band booked, consider creating an emergency backup playlist, asking a friend to bring their camera "just in case," etc.

Hopefully you won't have to use your backup plans. Most likely, you won't need them. It's a good idea to check up on your vendors and your DIY projects every once in a while before the big day so you can make sure that things are on schedule, or know if there's a potential problem brewing. And knowing that you have backup plans can give you a "safety net" and relieve a lot of stress. Let yourself make those backup plans and then do your best to forget about them and focus on everything going smoothly as planned.

The biggest unpredictable factor in a wedding is the weather, because it's the one thing we can't control. That's why it's so important to have a plan B, cross your fingers, and pray. If you're lucky, the weather will cooperate. If not, you'll be able to relax knowing you have a backup plan (and good wedding insurance, if you choose).

While the big elements of the wedding require backup plans, there will most likely be many small things that do not come together as planned. That's okay. It's to be expected, and it's all part of the wedding experience. If you can be flexible and stay calm, you can turn these bumps in the road into great wedding memories. In fact, many brides say that the most memorable and special parts of their wedding happened because things went wrong! So stay calm, stay positive, and know that whatever happens at your wedding will be amazing. The next chapter has lots of good advice on dealing with wedding-related stress and how to stay sane from the engagement to the big day itself.

Chapter 11
Letting off Steam

Life changes are stressful. Moving to a new home, getting married: these are all major milestones and transitions! Of course they are going to be stressful. The question is how you choose to cope with the stress. This chapter will give you ways to recognize if you are becoming over-stressed, and how to deal with it. You can also find some great ideas for stress relief at WeddingBrook.com.

Here are some signs that wedding planning is stressing you out:

- ✓ **You're skipping lunch to run wedding errands.** Forget about breakfast; you gave that up a long time ago!

- ✓ **Your fiancé starts talking about eloping.** And you can tell that he's serious.

- ✓ **Your relationship with your partner is taking a nosedive because you're too busy planning.** You conk out at night before he can even say, "Honey, are you in the mood for..."

- ✓ **You start questioning all of your wedding plans and decisions.** And then you question them again. And again.

- ✓ **You procrastinate with the things that really need to be done to focus on the little things.**
  Who knew that choosing a garter was so important?

- ✓ **Wedding planning stops being fun and starts being a burden.**

These are all signs that the wedding planning may be overshadowing everything else in your life. While planning a wedding is a big job, and an important one, maintaining a balance in your life is critical for staying sane and healthy. If you find yourself neglecting your friends and your partner, skipping meals, not sleeping, and dealing with wedding details all day long, it may be time to take a step back and reduce your stress level.

Stress is your body's normal response to threats and danger – the "fight-or-flight" reaction evolved to protect you. When you're in a truly dangerous situation, it helps you to stay focused and alert so that you can react appropriately. In a real emergency, the stress reaction can save your life. In important situations, like a big test or a presentation at work, stress keeps you on your toes and sharpens your concentration so that you perform at your best. So while most of us think of stress as a negative thing, in **certain situations** it's absolutely crucial.

But outside of these situations, stress stops being helpful and starts causing damage to your mental and physical well-being. Your body is not meant to sustain the stress response for long periods of time. And when you keep your mind and body in a high-stress state, you will start to feel the negative effects.

Physically, you may start to experience: headaches, muscle pain, chest pain, fatigue, low energy, changes in sex drive, upset stomach, changes in appetite, and insomnia or other sleep problems. You might start to feel anxious, restless, unmotivated, irritable, or depressed. You might find that you have a shorter fuse than normal. These are all warning signs that you need to lower the dial on your stress level.

So how can you take a chill pill and get away from all the wedding stress? First, you should make time every day to exercise, do yoga, or meditate. This is "you time," where you can re-center yourself and give your body a chance to recover and relax. Another good idea is to take "mini-breaks" when you start feeling overwhelmed.

Here's a three-minute exercise that has its roots in ancient yoga techniques that will help you relax: Find a comfortable place to sit with your back straight, but not tense. Sit cross-legged, and rest your hands on your knees. Now focus on breathing long, deep, and slow breaths, from your abdomen. Fill your lungs as much as you can, letting the breath push out your belly, then rise up into your chest. Hold it for a moment, then release that breath slowly and gently. Sit quietly, just focusing on your breathing, for two or three minutes. You'll be amazed at how relaxed and refreshed you feel afterwards!

Another technique, as silly as it may sound, is to make a list of positive affirmations that you can use to remind yourself what your wedding is all about. Give yourself a mantra that you can whisper under your breath whenever you feel your stress levels rising. For example: "Our wedding will be beautiful and special no matter what happens." How about, "It's about getting married; it's not about the flowers/decorations/catering/etc." Or, "The wedding is only one day, and then we will be married." Or even something simple like, "This is NOT a big deal."

Finally, be sure to schedule time to unwind with your fiancé, family, and friends. Your support network is what's going to get you through this wedding craziness, so be sure to set aside fun time. Here are some ideas to keep you relaxed and sane:

- ✓ **Go to a day spa and treat yourself** to a mani-pedi, massage, facial – the works! After all, you're a bride and you deserve to look beautiful and feel good. If you can convince your fiancé to come with you, a couples massage might be just the thing.

- ✓ Speaking of couples massages, **invest in some scented oils or lotions, and take turns giving and receiving massages with your partner**. Not only do you get to relax and de-stress, you also get some quality time with the love of your life.

- ✓ **Plan a girls' night out**... and *don't* talk about the wedding! Go out dancing or to a comedy club or a movie, and just be silly and have fun.

- ✓ **Turn your cell phone off and head out into the wilderness for some time communing with nature**. Go for a walk on the beach or in the woods, and let the sights and sounds of nature relax you.

- ✓ **Take time for family**. Stop by to have a cup of tea with Grandma and chat about nothing in particular. She'll appreciate the visit and you'll feel good knowing you made her so happy.

- ✓ **Cuddle up with a good book**. There's nothing like a good book to help you escape from reality for a little while. You might want to pick something light and fluffy that's easy to read, or you could tackle the epic novel that's been sitting on your shelf and gathering dust. Ask your friends for their recommendations. Nothing wedding-oriented, no self-help, nothing stressful in any way.

✓ **The play's the thing**. Find out what's going on in your neighborhood – a festival, play, concert, or jazz night can be a nice change of pace. Many of these events are also free, which is a huge plus when you're planning a wedding on a budget!

Even when you're doing all you can to stay sane and relaxed, wedding planning can be overwhelming. If you're lucky and go in with realistic expectations, it's possible that you'll make it through the whole process without breaking down in tears. But that's unlikely. It's more likely that you WILL have moments where you feel like throwing away all your spreadsheets and catching the next flight to Vegas. And that's okay. Weddings are hard, and it's okay to cry sometimes. Don't feel guilty about it, just let the tears come, and when you're finished, pick yourself up and keep going. Your feelings are valid, and you should never feel guilty for, or ashamed of, your emotions.

And that brings me to that ever-popular term: "Bridezilla." Our culture is obsessed with encouraging women to plan the "perfect" wedding, and then making them feel bad when they get stressed and frazzled about the details. It seems like a lose-lose situation. So when you feel like a "bridezilla," or someone has the nerve to use that term around you, just remember this: You're getting married. It's a major life transition. You're trying to throw an event that fulfills your dreams and keeps everyone else happy in the process. You should feel empowered to make the choices that are right for you. You're allowed to have opinions and make decisions. You're even allowed to get angry now and then. You're the one getting married, after all! The hardest part about wedding planning is there is almost always a conflict between what we hoped would be and what is. Sometimes we can roll with the punches and take things in stride, and sometimes the reality is disappointing.

When that happens, it's okay to cry a little and be upset... and then remind yourself just one more time what the wedding is really about.

One piece of advice that will help you stay sane is to give yourself a stress deadline. Pick a date, whether it's two days before the wedding or the day before, when you will stop stressing about the things that aren't done. If you haven't finished it the day before the wedding, it's not getting done. So give yourself permission to let it go and not worry about it anymore. Whatever it is, unless it's the groom, your wedding can and will go on without it.

On the wedding day itself, do your best to stay in the moment. This is your day – it's not your job to keep everyone else happy. As hard as this may sound, it's your job to just **let it go and walk away.** If you have bridesmaids, let them help you by forming a virtual (or physical) wall of defense around you. Their job is to let nothing upset you or stress you out. It's very common for family conflicts to arise at weddings. Emotions are running high, and the whole family is together in one place (most of the time with alcohol). The next chapter will talk about how to deal with the family conflicts that may arise during the planning process. But today, on your wedding day, they are not your responsibility. Your only job is to enjoy yourself, enjoy the moment, and get married!

Chapter 12
Coping with Conflicts

There's no doubt about it: weddings can be emotionally complicated. While the magazines make it look like wedding planning is all fun and checklists, the reality is often more difficult and complex. You are discussing heavy issues – beliefs, money, relationships – with the people you love. "Complicated" is an understatement! So how do you navigate the conflicts that arise between family members during the engagement and planning? How do you plan a wedding and plan for life *after* the wedding at the same time? With lots of patience, and a healthy dose of the magic word: **compromise.**

The engagement period isn't just the time to plan the wedding. It's valuable time that should be spent adjusting to the idea of forming a new family unit; it's a period of transition not just for you and your partner, but for your families as well. Don't expect that this transition will happen entirely smoothly and quietly (if it does, there's something wrong!). Conflicts and disagreements are to be expected at this stage, and it's much better to hash out the big issues now, rather than have them explode during or after the wedding, or after the birth of your first child. If you try to think of these conflicts as a step in the right direction (as silly as that might sound), it will change the way you approach them. Instead of just seeing the arguments as pointless fights, take a deep breath: Part of being engaged is learning how to set boundaries between your respective families and the new family you are creating with your partner. So when you find yourself stressing out because of these conflicts, remind yourself that each one brings you a little bit closer to defining your own new family.

At its core, a wedding is about joining two people from different households to create a new family – your family. But it's safe to say that your "old family" will have some opinions about the wedding plans, especially if they are contributing financially. Even with the most functional of families (and isn't every family dysfunctional in some way?), things tend to get hairy now and then as their ideas for your wedding conflict with the vision that you and your fiancé have agreed on. A solution may be to allow your families some control over aspects of the wedding that aren't as important to you. Once you and your partner have decided on **your** priorities, sit the families down (together or separately, whatever works best) and discuss the things that you're not willing to change. You can say something like, "Mom, Dad, we've discussed this and we really feel strongly that we'd like to have A, B, and C at our wedding. But we appreciate your input and value your opinions – so what do you think about D, E, and F?" Offering them a role in the process is a way to keep your families happy from the beginning.

It may also help to try to see things from your family's perspective. Sometimes a conflict may appear to be about a small thing on the surface, but underneath it is about something much more serious. For example, your mother may have very strong opinions about your wearing her wedding dress. But deep down, she's really feeling that she's losing her baby girl and having trouble letting go. The dress is just her way of expressing how emotional she is and how difficult this is for her. Your mom has probably been looking forward to your wedding longer than you have, and she has lots of mixed emotions about your getting married and starting a family of your own. Be patient, try to see things from her perspective, and – most importantly – communicate openly and honestly.

If conflicts arise with your future in-laws, let your partner try to calm the winds before you jump into the fray. Make it clear that you are making decisions together, but let him do the talking – he knows his family best. Handle conflicts on your side the same way. Present a united front, and make sure that your families understand that while you will always love them and will do your best to accommodate them, your loyalties are shifting now to your new family – and that's as it should be.

Some brides do approach wedding planning without their families. Sometimes your family may not want to be involved. Your relationship with them may be strained for whatever reason, or you may have lost one or both of your parents. Having an absent parent, emotionally or physically, is very hard and painful. You may feel cheated out of an experience that you've been dreaming about since you were little. It's okay to feel grief about that, and it's okay to cry. You're not overreacting at all. Next, do what you have to do to compensate. Maybe you have another close relative who'd be willing to stand in for your parent. Maybe you'll change the wedding plans to something that you feel more comfortable with. No matter how involved or uninvolved your family is, you need to do what's best for you emotionally.

What about your relationship with your fiancé as you plan this wedding together? You're planning a huge event, with lots of complicated logistics, plenty of details to organize, and a guest list involving your extended families. You're dealing with issues of faith, values, and money all at the same time. And you've probably never planned a project this big together. Does that sound like a recipe for stress, or what? And yet, while it may be daunting, it's also an incredible opportunity for you and your fiancé to bond and become closer than ever.

Here's something to keep in mind: your fiancé may be just as invested in the wedding plans as you are. He may have an opinion on every decision, and very definite ideas about how he wants things to go. But it's a lot more likely that he won't have an opinion on everything. In fact, his favorite sentence might be, "whatever you want to do, honey." And while this can be frustrating, take it in stride – it's okay if he doesn't care what color the flowers are, or what your bridesmaids are wearing. It doesn't mean he cares about the wedding any less than you do. It just means he's less invested in the details.

Remember, being engaged is not just about planning a wedding. It's about planning your life together **after** the wedding. And here's where it's important to sit down and have some serious talks about the kind of life you envision together. This can happen in the framework of premarital counseling if you feel comfortable with that option.

We all have beliefs and values that are important to us. Your partner may share all of those values with you, but it's more likely that you'll have some differences. Confronting this reality, putting everything on the table, and eventually learning to compromise – *especially* when it's complicated – will make you a stronger, happier couple during this period of transition and into the future. Maybe these topics have come up in discussions before. Maybe you've avoided talking about them because they're difficult. Maybe you've been living together for so long that they're not an issue anymore. But here are some things that you should be talking and thinking about as you envision life after the wedding:

- ✓ **What does the future look like?**

- ✓ **Where will you live?** The country, the city, or the suburbs? Where do you picture your life together?

- ✓ **How will you handle merging your finances?** Do you have a savings plan set up? What are your assets and liabilities (including debt)? What are your financial goals? How will you afford the lifestyle you want?

- ✓ **What career goals do you each have?** How will family fit into those careers?

- ✓ **What other goals do you have?**

- ✓ **What if one of you got a great job across the country?**

- ✓ **What faith backgrounds do each of you come from and how will they merge?** What will religious practice or faith look like in your household, if it exists at all?

- ✓ **How will you approach the issue of religion if/when you have kids?** What holidays will you celebrate (if any) and how?

- ✓ **Do you want kids?** How many? Why or why not?

- ✓ **What if you can't have kids?** Would you consider adoption?

- ✓ **What kind of parent do you want to be?** How will you share the parenting duties?

- ✓ **What kind of relationships will you have with your families?** How often will you visit? Would you consider living near family?

- ✓ **How do you plan to divide up the household responsibilities?** What happens if you feel that the other isn't pulling their weight?

- ✓ **Do you have similar standards for being organized and clean?** If not, how can you meet in the middle?

- ✓ **What happens when you each get upset/offended/angry?** How do you react? Make a plan for approaching conflicts and solving problems.

- ✓ **What about one's personal family history does the other need to know before going into marriage?** How does each of your parents' history affect how you view marriage? How do you feel about divorce? How do you feel about couples counseling?

- ✓ **Are there any difficult topics that you've never shared?** Do you have traumas in your past, or issues with addiction/past relationships/abuse?

Many of these questions may be difficult to talk about. But, just as with family conflicts, it's better to put these issues on the table during the engagement than to have them pop up a year or two (or ten, or twenty) into your marriage.

It's also a good idea to talk about the logistical minutiae of "after the wedding" to make sure you and your fiancé are on the same page. For example, do you plan to change your name? Who's going to handle the thank-yous and the after-the-wedding arrangements? What else needs to be done before you can start settling in as a married couple? Make planning for your marriage a part of the wedding plans. After all, the wedding is only one day, but you will be married for many years to come.

Chapter 13
Surviving (and Enjoying!) the Big Day

It's the big day, and we've come full circle. You've done all the planning, written the checklists (and the checks), and appointed your wedding managers. Now that everything's planned, it's time to go back to the beginning, to the lists you made at the very beginning of the process. Remember your "big dream" and "non-negotiable" lists? Look at those one more time and remind yourself of the things that are most important to you about this wedding. And remind yourself of *the* most important thing – you're getting married to the person you love!

Here are some practical day-of tips to help you stay calm, energized, and enjoy the day as much as possible:

If you have a regular morning routine, stick with it as much as you can. Whether it's yoga, a quick run or exercise routine, or just your morning coffee and the paper, do it! The regular routine will help calm your nerves and start the day off right.

Even if you don't normally eat breakfast, today is one day that you'll want to! Something low-fat and non-greasy like cereal, yogurt, scrambled eggs, or toast with a piece of fruit will work well. Avoid orange juice or other acidic foods that may irritate your stomach. Don't eat too much, and store some snacks like granola bars or dried fruit in your bag to keep your energy up during the day. Be sure to drink lots of water – even though it means multiple trips to the bathroom in the middle of hair and makeup, it's a lot better than the alternative: being dehydrated and not feeling well at the wedding itself.

You've already given yourself a no-stress deadline and put your trust in your wedding managers – and that means you no longer have to worry about the things that can go wrong, or what you can do about them. Little things *do* go wrong at every wedding. Someone will probably forget something. The weather may not cooperate. Things may go missing. I'm not telling you this to worry you; I'm saying it because it's true, and also because it ultimately doesn't matter. If you can be flexible and stay relaxed, you can take any bump in the road and turn it into a great wedding memory. Of course you'd love for everything to go as planned, but if it doesn't, your wedding will still be memorable, unique, and amazing.

Before you start your walk down the aisle, close your eyes and take a deep breath. Open them and look around: Take in the beautiful setting, the flowers and decorations, and the faces of your friends and family gathered together. Let yourself be in the moment; it will all be over in a flash. Let go of all the details that you were so worried about just a few days ago. There's nothing you can do about them now. This is your moment, this is the reason you're here: to make a lifelong commitment to the person you love.

I highly recommend taking some time after the ceremony to be alone with your new husband, even if it's just 15 minutes to grab a bite to eat, relax, and enjoy each other's company as a married couple by yourselves. This is a very special time that you will cherish afterwards – your first few moments of marriage. Then get out on the dance floor, greet all your friends and family, and enjoy the party!

You may not feel like you expected to feel at your wedding. You may feel somewhat detached from your body. You may feel like time is going way too fast and suddenly it's over. You may only remember flashes here and there. Or you may remember every single moment with perfect clarity. You can try to set the mood with music and décor, but ultimately you have no idea how you will feel until you are there. Whatever those feelings are, embrace them. Forget about how the decorations look and whether the cake turned out the way you wanted. Focus on yourself and your partner, and on sharing your joy with your loved ones. Stop thinking and just let yourself **feel** as much as possible. This is the day you've invested so much time and energy planning for – now it's time to let yourself be the bride and enjoy the fruits of your hard work.

If you don't have that amazing feeling of joy that you think you're "supposed" to have, that's okay, too. It may hit you later, after the wedding, just how much you enjoyed yourself and what a great day it was. And even if it doesn't, remember that your wedding **isn't** the biggest day of your life; it's only the beginning.

Epilogue – You Can Do This!

From the start of your engagement to the honeymoon, this is one of the most exciting times of your life – and one of the most stressful. But if you take one thing away from this book , I hope it's that you can plan a wedding that's fun, elegant, budget-friendly and right for you as a couple – and without doing everything the wedding industry says you "must" do. Sure, it takes some creative thinking, and you won't be able to do it on your own, but the result will be something totally unique and special.

Planning a wedding is great practice for married life. Just like your wedding, your marriage can be what you and your husband want it to be. It's something that you create together and re-create every single day. Marriage means that you're stronger together than you are apart. Marriage enables, and sometimes even forces us to become our best selves.

This is my wish for you: that your wedding is just the first day of your wonderful married life, and that you have many happy years together to come.

Congratulations!

About the Author

Sarah Brookhaven is a work-from-home, homeschool mom who loves all things artistic, crafty, and yes, even geeky. Sarah found that her interest in art and her natural attention to detail and organization (probably from her engineering background) were a "match made in heaven" – at least where wedding planning was concerned. She began to research current wedding trends in 2011 and was shocked to discover how expensive and overwhelming the wedding planning process had become:

"I couldn't believe what I found. When I was married back in 1988, it was so much simpler – more laid back and definitely less expensive!"

Sarah searched high and low for wedding bargains and decided to share her discoveries with other women, hoping to relieve some of the stress and expense that go along with planning a wedding. She created WeddingBrook.com as a newsy and helpful wedding website that's fun to read and share.

Look for more wedding planning books by Sarah as she continues her research and her discoveries. And feel free to check out WeddingBrook.com for all the latest news and trends. If you have any suggestions for Sarah, please drop her a note at Sarah@WeddingBrook.com. She would love to hear from you!

Printed in Great Britain
by Amazon.co.uk, Ltd.,
Marston Gate.